PIANO · VOCAL · GUITAR

Y0-AAR-010

# Country Women

## ▼ OF THE 90'S ▼

Let your love flow

ISBN 0-7935-2052-5

HL® Hal Leonard Publishing Corporation
7777 West Bluemound Road P.O. Box 13819 Milwaukee, WI 53213

# ACES

Words and Music by
CHERYL WHEELER

# ASKING US TO DANCE

Words and Music by
HUGH PRESTWOOD

# BLUE ROSE IS

Words and Music by PAM TILLIS,
BOB DIPIERO and JAN BUCKINGHAM

# CHAINS

Words and Music by BUD RENEAU
and HAL BYNUM

**Moderate Country Rock**

Bought a tic-ket to Se-at-tle, but I can't get to the plane.
nev-er try to hold me till you see me walk-in' out. ___ I

Ev-ery-time I leave you I keep run-nin' out of chain.
guess you'd rath-er be with me than ev-er be with-out.
My hun-ger for your lov-in' nev-er
You call me back and kiss me and my

# DOWN AT THE TWIST AND SHOUT

Words and Music by
MARY-CHAPIN CARPENTER

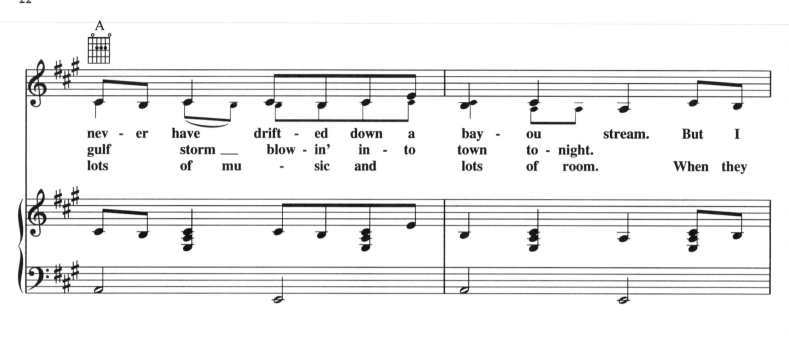

never have drift - ed down a bay - ou stream. But I
gulf storm ___ blow - in' in - to town to - night.
lots of mu - sic and lots of room. When they

heard that mu - sic on the ra - di - o, and I ___
Liv - in' on the del - ta it's quite ___ a show. ___ They got hur-
play you a waltz from a nine - teen ten, you're

swore some - day I was gon - na go: ___ down a - high - way 10, past a-
- ri - cane par - ties ev - 'ry time it blows. ___ But here up north ___ it's a
gon - na feel a lit - tle bit young a - gain. ___ Well you learn to dance ___ with your

wait - ing there _ who used to know me well. _ I'm go - ing

I'm gon - na

I'm go - ing

out to - night _ to find _ my - self _ a friend. _

# THE GREATEST MAN I NEVER KNEW

Words and Music by RICHARD LEIGH
and LAYNG MARTINE, JR.

The great-est man I_____ nev - er knew\_\_ lived just down the hall,
The great-est man I_____ nev - er knew\_\_ came home late ev - 'ry night,
The great-est words I_____ nev - er heard\_\_ I guess I'll nev - er hear.

34

# MAYBE IT WAS MEMPHIS

Words and Music by
MICHAEL ANDERSON

To Coda

Mem- phis, _____ may - be it was South-ern \_\_ sum-mer nights. \_\_ May-be it was

you, \_ may-be it was me, but it sure felt right. _____

# I FEEL LUCKY

Words and Music by MARY-CHAPIN CARPENTER
and DON SCHLITZ

woke up this morn - ing, stum - bled out of my rack. ___ I o -
strolled down to the cor - ner, gave my num - bers to the clerk. The pot's
lev - en mil - lion lat - er, I was sit - tin' at the bar. I bought ___

E7

B7

F#7

# LONESOME STANDARD TIME

Words and Music by LARRY CORDLE
and JIM RUSHING

**D.S. al Coda**
(Take 2nd ending)

There's a

**CODA**

Well, if you shud-der at the mu - sic ___ of a

hoot owl in the pines, ___

# NO ONE ELSE ON EARTH

Words and Music by SAM LORBER,
STEWART HARRIS and JILL COLUCCI

# OH WHAT IT DID TO ME

Words and Music by
JERRY CRUTCHFIELD

held_____ you ten - der - ly._____
nough \_\_\_\_\_ for all \_\_\_\_\_ three. _____
like they used to be. _____

You say\_\_\_\_\_ when she held \_\_\_\_\_ you it did
You
That

noth-ing\_\_\_\_\_ to _____ you, but oh, what it

did\_\_ to_____ me. You

# RUMOR HAS IT

Words and Music by LARRY SHELL,
VERN DANT and BRUCE BURCH

# PUT YOURSELF IN MY PLACE

Words and Music by CARL JACKSON
and PAM TILLIS

# SHAKE THE SUGAR TREE

Words and Music by
CHAPIN HARTFORD

shake _____ the sug-ar tree._

To Coda

An-oth- er night and you're sleep - in',

I'm a-wake and I'm dream - in', oh Hon-ey, 'bout the way that it

used to be._ A lit - tle time's gone by, do you

# SHE IS HIS ONLY NEED

Words and Music by
DAVE LOGGINS

**With a relaxed feel**

Bil - ly was a small town lon - er __ who nev - er did dream __ of ev - er leav-ing south-ern Ar - i - zo - na __ or ev - er hear-ing wed-ding bells __ ring.

# SOME KIND OF TROUBLE

Words and Music by BRENT MAHER,
DON POTTER and MIKE REID

Late one night I heard a knock on my door. ___ No sur-prise ___ it was

# TAKE IT LIKE A MAN

Words and Music by
TONY HASELDEN

# TIME PASSES BY

Words and Music by JON VEZNER
and SUSAN LONGACRE

do what __ we like __ and love while __ we're here _____ be - fore___

___ time pass - es __ by.

# THAT'S WHAT I LIKE ABOUT YOU

Words and Music by JOHN HADLEY,
KEVIN WELCH and WALLY WILSON

# WATCH ME

Words and Music by GARY BURR<br/>and TOM SHAPIRO

**MCA** music publishing

# WHERE'VE YOU BEEN

Words and Music by DON HENRY
and JON VEZNER

# (WITHOUT YOU)
# WHAT DO I DO WITH ME

Words and Music by DAVID LEWIS,
ROYCE PORTER and DAVID CHAMBERLAIN

# THE WOMAN BEFORE ME

Words and Music by
JUDE JOHNSTONE

To Coda

Some-times I think __ you must be talk - in' to __ the wom-an be - fore __ me __ and you. __

Some - times in an __

If there are sor - rows that bring ____ back a tear, ____

don't let them keep ___ us a - part. ____

# YOU LIE

Words and Music by AUSTIN ROBERTS,
BOBBY FISCHER and CHARLIE BLACK

**Moderate country waltz**

We lie in the dark. ___ I
Des-p'rate to talk, ___
How long un-til ___ you

know you're a-wake. ___ The on-ly sounds ___ are the
yearn-ing to touch, ___ burn-ing in-side ___ 'cause I
just can't go ___ on, and the urge to break ___ loose is